Dear Parents and Educators,

Welcome to Penguin Young Readers! As parents and educators, you know that each child develops at his or her own pace—in terms of speech, critical thinking, and, of course, reading. Penguin Young Readers recognizes this fact. As a result, each Penguin Young Readers book is assigned a traditional easy-to-read level (1–4) as well as a Guided Reading Level (A–P). Both of these systems will help you choose the right book for your child. Please refer to the back of each book for specific leveling information. Penguin Young Readers features esteemed authors and illustrators, stories about favorite characters, fascinating nonfiction, and more!

## Amazing Arctic Animals

LEVEL **3**

GUIDED READING LEVEL **L**

This book is perfect for a **Transitional Reader** who:
• can read multisyllable and compound words;
• can read words with prefixes and suffixes;
• is able to identify story elements (beginning, middle, end, plot, setting, characters, problem, solution); and
• can understand different points of view.

Here are some **activities** you can do during and after reading this book:
• Vocabulary: Some of the words in this book may be unfamiliar. Find each of the words below in the text. Use a dictionary to look up any words you do not understand.

| adaptations | huddle | predators | protective | talons |
| blubber | migration | prey | sly | tundra |

• Writing: The author uses text boxes, like the one on page 19 called "All about the polar bear," to give additional facts. Pretend you are the author and your editor has asked you to delete the text boxes. Pick one or two text boxes and rewrite the information in paragraph form.

Remember, sharing the love of reading with a child is the best gift you can give!

—Bonnie Bader, EdM
  Penguin Young Readers program

*Penguin Young Readers are leveled by independent reviewers applying the standards developed by Irene Fountas and Gay Su Pinnell in *Matching Books to Readers: Using Leveled Books in Guided Reading*, Heinemann, 1999.

To Evan, Jacob, and Abby—JG

To all my family, near and far—LB

Penguin Young Readers
Published by the Penguin Group
Penguin Group (USA) Inc., 375 Hudson Street, New York, New York 10014, USA
Penguin Group (Canada), 90 Eglinton Avenue East, Suite 700, Toronto, Ontario M4P 2Y3, Canada
(a division of Pearson Penguin Canada Inc.)
Penguin Books Ltd, 80 Strand, London WC2R 0RL, England
Penguin Ireland, 25 St Stephen's Green, Dublin 2, Ireland (a division of Penguin Books Ltd)
Penguin Group (Australia), 707 Collins Street, Melbourne, Victoria 3008, Australia
(a division of Pearson Australia Group Pty Ltd)
Penguin Books India Pvt Ltd, 11 Community Centre, Panchsheel Park, New Delhi—110 017, India
Penguin Group (NZ), 67 Apollo Drive, Rosedale, Auckland 0632, New Zealand
(a division of Pearson New Zealand Ltd)
Penguin Books, Rosebank Office Park, 181 Jan Smuts Avenue, Parktown North 2193, South Africa
Penguin China, B7 Jaiming Center, 27 East Third Ring Road North,
Chaoyang District, Beijing 100020, China

Penguin Books Ltd, Registered Offices: 80 Strand, London WC2R 0RL, England

Library of Congress Control Number: 2002004662

ISBN 978-0-448-42844-4                          10 9 8 7 6 5

PENGUIN YOUNG READERS

LEVEL 3
TRANSITIONAL READER

# AMAZING ARCTIC ANIMALS

by Jackie Glassman
illustrated by Lisa Bonforte

Penguin Young Readers
An Imprint of Penguin Group (USA) Inc.

# The Chilliest Place on Earth

Grab your hat and scarf.

Pull on your boots and mittens.

You are about to enter one of the chilliest places on earth—the Arctic!

Home to the North Pole, the Arctic is a very cold place. It is made up of an ice-covered sea and a cold, treeless desert. The treeless desert is called the tundra.

In the Arctic, the winter lasts for six months.

That's half the year.

Even summertime is chilly in the Arctic.

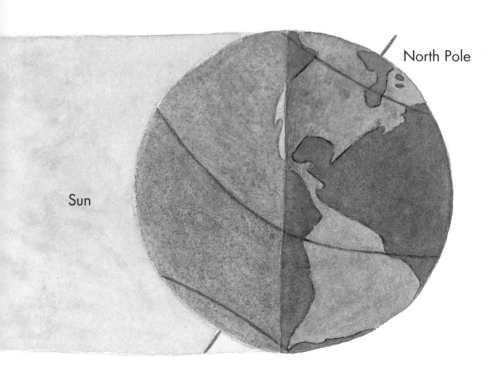

North Pole

Sun

Arctic winters are dark. That's because in the winter, the northern part of the Earth tilts away from the sun.

Can you imagine six months without any sunshine?

Lots of animals visit the Arctic during the summer.

Birds called **terns** fly here from as far away as the Antarctic. That's on the other side of the world!

Thousands of deer called **caribou** walk to the tundra from the Arctic's forests.

But only a few animals dare to stay for the long, cold winter. Most return to warmer places.

The brave animals that stay all year have special ways to survive cold Arctic winters. These ways are called adaptations.

Arctic birds are covered from head to toe in a snowsuit of feathers. A soft layer next to their skin called down keeps them warm. Outer feathers keep them dry.

Arctic animals keep warm because they have lots of thick fur. Their fur coats keep them warm the same way that wearing a coat keeps you warm when it's cold outside.

Some Arctic animals, like **whales**, have a thick layer of fat under their skin. This fat is called blubber.

Blubber keeps animals warm
even when they swim in
the icy Arctic Ocean.

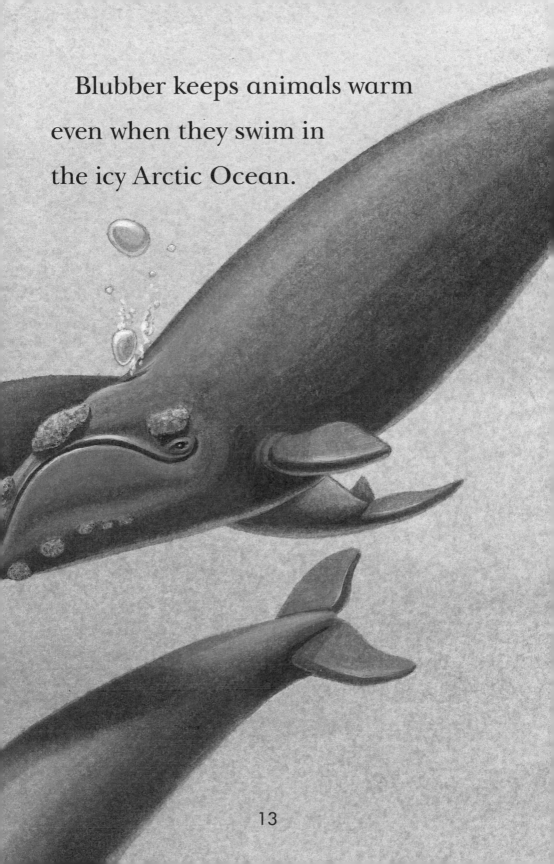

Fur, fat, and feathers are just a few
of the Arctic animals' adaptations.
Each animal has its own special way
of living in the coldest place on earth.

Who are these creatures, and
how do they adapt to the harsh
Arctic winter?

Let's find out.

# By Land

Who is the largest land-living animal in the Arctic? The **polar bear**!

He loves to swim in the freezing
water and roll in the snow.

His big, furry coat and thick layer
of fat keep him nice and warm.

The polar bear is a great hunter. He has very strong paws. He can kill a seal with just one swat! Seals are a polar bear's favorite dinner.

The polar bear's wide paws help him walk on the snow without sinking in. His furry soles help keep him from slipping on the ice.

## All about the polar bear

| | |
|---|---|
| **Baby name:** | cub |
| **Size at birth:** | 1½ pounds, 1 foot tall |
| **Size full-grown:** | 1,000–2,200 pounds (males) |
| | 300–900 pounds (females) |
| **Favorite foods:** | seals, fish, birds, eggs, seaweed, |
| | berries, garbage (yuck!) |
| **Enemies:** | killer whales, walruses, humans |

The sly **arctic fox** is hard to see.

In winter, her gray-brown coat turns

thick and white to match the snow.

Watch as she quietly follows

a polar bear to steal his kill.

The arctic fox doesn't mind the cold. Her small, furry body and tiny ears keep in body heat. Her bushy tail wraps around her like a blanket while she sleeps.

## All about the arctic fox

| | |
|---|---|
| **Baby name:** | kit |
| **Size at birth:** | 2½–5 ounces |
| **Size full-grown:** | 6–17 pounds |
| **Favorite foods:** | birds, bird eggs, berries, fish, small mammals |
| **Enemies:** | humans, polar bears |

**Arctic hares** huddle together to stay warm.

Oh no! Here comes a wolf.

The hares quickly hop away.

The arctic hare has big feet. These big feet act like snowshoes. They help the hares run on top of the snow without falling in it. This makes it easy for them to get away from predators.

# All about the arctic hare

| | |
|---|---|
| **Baby name:** | leveret |
| **Size at birth:** | 2 ounces |
| **Size full-grown:** | 9–12 pounds, 22–28 inches long |
| **Favorite foods:** | willow leaves, willow shoots, willow bark, willow roots, grasses, herbs, flowers |
| **Enemies of adult arctic hares:** | arctic foxes, wolves, humans |
| **Enemies of young arctic hares:** | gyrfalcons, snowy owls, ermines |

Here comes the huge **muskox**!
His long, furry coat keeps him
cozy and warm. Underneath all that
hair is a layer of wool to keep out
cold Arctic air.

When a wolf is near, the protective muskoxen make a ring around their calves.

With horns facing out, they are ready to charge the enemy.

## All about the muskox

| | |
|---|---|
| **Baby name:** | calf |
| **Size at birth:** | 22–31 pounds |
| **Size full-grown:** | (bull) 600–800 pounds, 5 feet tall at shoulder (cow) 400–500 pounds, 4 feet tall at shoulder |
| **Favorite foods:** | grass, bushes, some arctic flowers |
| **Enemies:** | wolves, polar bears |

Don't be scared of the big, bad wolf. She only hunts to get food. She almost never attacks people.

Good eyes and a strong sense of smell help the wolf hunt for prey.

Baby **arctic wolves** can't see or hear. They rely on their mother to feed and protect them.

## All about the arctic wolf

| | |
|---|---|
| **Baby name:** | pup |
| **Size at birth:** | 11–18 ounces, 6–8 inches long |
| **Size full-grown:** | 50–175 pounds |
| **Favorite foods:** | arctic hares, lemmings, caribou, moose, muskoxen |
| **Enemies:** | humans |

# By Sea

Splash! The **ringed seal** dives into the icy, cold sea.

A thick layer of blubber keeps him warm. This fat makes up almost half his weight.

The seal can stay underwater for almost an hour without even taking a breath.

His big, round eyes help him see in the dark water.

## All about the ringed seal

| | |
|---|---|
| **Baby name:** | pup |
| **Size at birth:** | 8–11 pounds, 2 feet long |
| **Size full-grown:** | 130–155 pounds, 5 feet long |
| **Favorite foods:** | shrimp, crabs, arctic cod (fish), squid |
| **Enemies:** | polar bears, killer whales, humans |

Who is the giant of the sea with teeth as long as your arms?

The **walrus**, of course!

The walrus's two big teeth are called tusks.

The walrus hooks her tusks into the ice to pull herself out of the water. That is why she is nicknamed "the tooth walker."

The walrus uses her whiskers to feel for clams on the ocean floor. A hungry walrus can eat up to 6,000 clams a day!

Walruses like to stay close to one another. Huddling together keeps them warm.

As a group, they protect their babies from polar bears and killer whales.

## All about the walrus

| | |
|---|---|
| **Baby name:** | calf |
| **Size at birth:** | 99–165 pounds, 4 feet long |
| **Size full-grown:** | 1,700–3,400 pounds, 9–12 feet long (males) 900–2,700 pounds, 7–10 feet long (females) |
| **Favorite foods:** | arctic cod, sea cucumbers, clams, crabs, snails, worms |
| **Enemies:** | polar bears, killer whales, humans |

There is nothing fishy about whales.
That's because they are mammals!

To breathe, they must come up for
air. Whales take in air through a
small hole on the top of their heads.

Nicknamed "sea canaries," **beluga whales** love to sing. They use sound to talk to one another and to find prey.

## All about the beluga whale

| | |
|---|---|
| **Baby name:** | calf |
| **Size at birth:** | 90–130 pounds, 5 feet long |
| **Size full-grown:** | 1,000–3,000 pounds, 12–15 feet long |
| **Favorite foods:** | crabs, clams, squid, fish, shrimp, octopuses |
| **Enemies:** | polar bears, killer whales, humans, sharks |

# By Air

Do you see a white-feathered bird hiding in the snow?

It is a **ptarmigan** (say: TAR-mi-gun). He is hiding from his enemies.

When spring comes, the ptarmigan's feathers change color. Now they are brown, yellow, and white to match the grasses and melting snow.

Can you find this sneaky bird now?

## All about the ptarmigan

**Baby name:**       chick
**Size at birth:**   ½–13 ounces
**Size full-grown:** 10½ ounces–1½ pounds,
                     11–12 inches
**Favorite foods:**  berries, leaves, seeds, insects,
                     spiders, moss, buds
**Enemies:**         gyrfalcons, humans, snowy owls

*Whooo!* Who? Who has feathers
from nose to toes?

The **snowy owl**!

Her feathery snowsuit protects
her from the chilly Arctic winds.

Flying high in the sky, the snowy owl spots prey far below. She has very good eyesight and hearing.

*Whoosh!* She swoops down, grabs dinner with her sharp, curved claws, and brings it back to her nest.

## All about the snowy owl

| | |
|---|---|
| **Baby name:** | owlet |
| **Size at birth:** | ¾ ounce |
| **Size full-grown:** | 3½–4½ pounds, 20–27 inches |
| **Favorite foods:** | arctic hares, lemmings, ptarmigan, mice |
| **Enemies:** | arctic foxes, arctic wolves |

Other animals hide in fear when the mighty **gyrfalcon** (say: JUHR-fal-kehn) comes near. His strong talons, or claws, and powerful eyesight make this giant bird a great hunter.

The gyrfalcon is so fast, he can catch a bird in mid-flight. He knocks down his prey with his powerful beak.

## All about the gyrfalcon

**Baby name:** chick
**Size at birth:** 1–1½ pounds
**Size full-grown:** 2½–4½ pounds
**Favorite foods:** ptarmigan, arctic hares, large ducks, geese, arctic ground squirrels
**Enemies:** arctic foxes, humans, wolverines

# Springtime!

After months of darkness, the sun finally begins to rise over the Arctic. As ice on the tundra melts, plants begin to grow and insect eggs hatch.

Suddenly there is lots of food for everyone.

Animal visitors from faraway places fly and walk many miles to come enjoy the tundra's feast!

Herds of caribou make the long
journey north from the Arctic forests.
It is the longest migration made by
any land animal. On the way,
they give birth to new calves.

When they finally reach the tundra, caribou eat everything in sight.

When winter comes, and their food is scarce, the fat stored in their bodies gives them needed energy.

## All about the caribou

**Baby name:**        calf
**Size at birth:**     10–26 pounds, 16 inches
**Size full-grown:** 175–700 pounds
**Favorite foods:**  grass, moss, lichens, mushrooms
**Enemies:**           wolves, bears, humans

Here come the terns.

They may be small, but these strong birds fly all the way from the Antarctic—that's over 12,000 miles!

Here on the sunny tundra, they make their nests and raise their babies.

In the fall, the terns will fly back halfway across the world.

They will arrive in the Antarctic—the other pole of the earth—just as the sun is rising there.

## All about the arctic tern

**Baby name:** chick
**Size at birth:** ½ ounce
**Size full-grown:** 2 pounds, 12–15 inches
**Favorite foods:** small fish, shrimp, krill, insects, small invertebrates
**Enemies:** humans

Summer in the Arctic is short.

Soon the sun will set, and the dark chill of winter will return.